JOHN LASSETER

Director of *Toy Story*

Lee Slater

Checkerboard Library

An Imprint of Abdo Publishing
abdopublishing.com

ABDOPUBLISHING.COM

Published by Abdo Publishing, a division of ABDO, PO Box 398166, Minneapolis, Minnesota 55439. Copyright © 2017 by Abdo Consulting Group, Inc. International copyrights reserved in all countries. No part of this book may be reproduced in any form without written permission from the publisher. Checkerboard Library™ is a trademark and logo of Abdo Publishing.

Printed in the United States of America, North Mankato, Minnesota

062016
092016

THIS BOOK CONTAINS
RECYCLED MATERIALS

Design: Christa Schneider, Mighty Media, Inc.
Production: Mighty Media, Inc.
Editor: Paige Polinsky
Cover Photograph: AP Images
Interior Photographs: Alamy, pp. 7, 25; AP Images, pp. 21, 29; Everett Collection NYC, pp. 13, 17, 19, 22; Getty Images, p. 11, 15; Shutterstock, pp. 5, 25, 27, 29; Yearbook Library, pp. 9, 28

Publishers Cataloging-in-Publication Data

Names: Slater, Lee, author.
Title: John Lasseter : director of Toy Story / by Lee Slater.
Description: Minneapolis, MN : Abdo Publishing, [2017] | Series: Movie makers | Includes index.
Identifiers: LCCN 2016934268 | ISBN 9781680781830 (lib. bdg.) | ISBN 9781680775686 (ebook)
Subjects: LCSH: Lasseter, John--Juvenile literature. | Motion picture producers and directors--United States--Biography--Juvenile literature. | Animators--United States--Biography--Juvenile literature. | Pixar (Firm)
Classification: DDC 791.4302/33/092 [B]--dc23
LC record available at /http://lccn.loc.gov/2016934268

CONTENTS

TOY STORY TRENDSETTER

A cowboy and a spaceman are strapped to a blazing rocket. They soar high into the sky as the fuse burns down. Seconds before explosion, the spaceman spreads his wings to escape.

This thrilling **scene** is from *Toy Story*, the first full-length computer-**animated** film. *Toy Story* amazed viewers at its 1995 release. That was thanks to writer and **director** John Lasseter.

Lasseter is creative chief and executive **producer** for both Pixar and Walt Disney Animation Studios. He oversees the creativity and quality of each film. Under his direction, *Toy Story*'s characters came to life.

Toy Story was just the beginning. Lasseter wrote and directed a **sequel**, *Toy Story 2*, **premiering** in 1999. The film was another hit! Lasseter was also a writer for 2010's award-winning *Toy Story 3*.

John Lasseter poses with action figures of characters Buzz (*left*) and Woody (*right*) at the world premiere of *Toy Story 3* in Hollywood, California.

Lasseter never outgrew his love of toys and great stories. In 2015, he announced that he would be **directing** *Toy Story 4*. The film is set to **premiere** in 2017. In one interview, Lasseter said, "I am very excited to be directing again. The story is . . . a brand new chapter in the Toy Story world."

CARTOON KID

John Alan Lasseter was born in Hollywood, California, on January 12, 1957. He arrived six minutes after his **twin** sister, Johanna. Their parents were Paul and Jewell Lasseter. Paul worked at a car **dealership**. Jewell was an art teacher. Both parents would influence and inspire John.

While growing up in Whittier, California, John loved drawing. His mother gave him plenty of art supplies. She even brought drawing paper to church to keep John busy. When he ran out of paper, he drew in the church songbooks. He made moving pictures with the page corners.

FAST FACT

John's parents only learned they were having twins a week before their birth. John's dad called John the "bonus baby."

John loved Disney's *Dumbo* as a child. It remains his favorite film of all time.

Although he loved drawing, John's favorite activity was watching cartoons. He woke up at 6:30 a.m. every Saturday and watched cartoons for hours. All of that time was well spent. His **passion** for cartoons would combine with his love for drawing. Together they would inspire him to become an **animator**.

INSPIRED
BY DISNEY

In ninth grade, John found a book called *The Art of* **Animation**. It explored the making of Walt Disney Studio's film *Sleeping Beauty.* While reading the book, John was surprised to learn that people made cartoons for a living.

John began writing to Walt Disney Studios. In 1973, the company invited him for a tour! John was fascinated by the animation department. The department manager encouraged John to study art when he went to college.

John **enrolled** at Pepperdine University after high school. But Walt Disney Studios soon sent him a letter. The company invited John to apply for a new animation program. The program was held at the California Institute of the Arts (CalArts) in Valencia. John applied immediately. He was the second person accepted.

John was voted Most Artistic his senior year of high school.

CLASSES AND
RIVER RIDES

When **animation** school began, Lasseter was thrilled to meet his peers and teachers. Some of Walt Disney Studios' greatest animators taught the classes. And the other students were as **passionate** about animation as Lasseter.

At CalArts, Lasseter learned traditional animation. Students worked with pencils, paper, and cameras. Lasseter quickly earned a reputation for creating great stories and characters. He won two Student **Academy Awards** for his short films.

Lasseter learned outside of the classroom too. He worked at nearby amusement park Disneyland as a Jungle Cruise guide. The river ride took guests past tropical ruins and wild animals. Leading the tour improved John's storytelling skills. He learned about delivery, timing, and adjusting **lines** when necessary.

A Jungle Cruise boat similar to the one Lasseter guided. Lasseter once said, "I would still be a Jungle Cruise skipper if I didn't get hired as an animator at Disney."

A DREAM COME TRUE?

CHAPTER 5

In 1979, Lasseter graduated from CalArts and applied for a job at Walt Disney Studios. Disney hired him and a few of his peers as **animators**. Lasseter's friend Glen Keane was one of them. Lasseter's future looked bright! But working at Disney was not what Lasseter had dreamed it would be.

A group of early Walt Disney animators advised the new animation team. Lasseter was excited to learn from these experienced artists. But they often rejected the new animators' ideas. Lasseter and his peers felt bored and unappreciated.

Lasseter and Keane were interested in computer **technology**. In 1983, the pair started their own project. They made a short film based on the children's book *Where the Wild Things Are*. The film used both computer-animation and hand-drawn characters.

Lasseter helped animate *The Fox and the Hound*. But the chief animators rejected his ideas for improving the movie's story and characters.

Lasseter and Keane **pitched** the idea to their bosses. But Disney executives were looking for faster, cheaper films. This project was neither. Soon after the pitch, Lasseter was fired.

THE SUPER
COMPUTER

Out of a job at Walt Disney Studios, Lasseter began looking for other work. But his search didn't last long. Lasseter soon received a job offer from Lucasfilm.

Lucasfilm was a production company created by **director** George Lucas. Lasseter had once visited the studio. There, he had met Ed Catmull, a computer scientist for the company. Catmull now offered Lasseter a position at Lucasfilm. Lasseter eagerly accepted the job.

Lucasfilm's employees were the brightest people Lasseter had ever met. He thought if anyone could shape the future of film, they could. Lasseter was part of a small research team that tested new **computer graphics**. One of their products was the Pixar Image Computer. It combined live film with **special effects**.

Lasseter draws on a digital tablet at Lucasfilm in 1985. The tablet transferred images directly to Lasseter's computer.

In 1984, Lasseter used the Pixar Image Computer to help develop a short film called "Adventures of André and Wally B." At its first **screening**, the viewers were stunned. The film had advanced **3-D** backgrounds and the first ever use of blurred motion! Members of the movie industry were impressed by this new **technology**. The future of **animation** was off and running.

PIXAR PIONEERS

In 1986, computer pioneer Steve Jobs bought Lucasfilm's Computer Division. Lasseter joined Catmull at the new company. Its name was Pixar. The company sold Pixar Image Computers and computer-related products.

Lasseter developed **animations** to display Pixar's **technology**. His 1986 short film "Luxo Jr." won an **Academy Award**, or Oscar, nomination. In 1988, Lasseter **directed** "Tin Toy." It won an Oscar for Best Animated Short Film. That same year, Lasseter married Nancy Tague, a **computer graphics engineer**.

Lasseter was living his dream. But making films cost Pixar too much money. The company struggled financially for years. Then, in 1991, Pixar received a proposal for a major project. And Lasseter's talent was a key part of the deal.

Jobs (*left*) greatly inspired Lasseter (*right*). He encouraged
Lasseter and the original Pixar team to do their very best.

TOY STORY
AND BEYOND!

Disney wanted to hire Pixar to make a full-length computer-**animated** film. Walt Disney Studios would own and release the film. But it wanted Lasseter's storytelling genius behind it all. Lasseter saw the deal as a great opportunity. In 1991, Pixar and Walt Disney Studios agreed to make three films together.

Toy Story was released four years later. It was a film sensation! The movie earned three **Academy Award** nominations. It proved that computer **technology** was not limited to short films. This was a huge step forward for animation.

Pixar's success grew. Lasseter **codirected** 2001's *Monsters, Inc.* He also oversaw 2003's *Finding Nemo.* This was Pixar's first film to win an Oscar for Best Animated Feature. Pixar's animation kept improving, but the films' stories remained most important.

Lasseter (*front right*) works on *Toy Story*. In 1996, Lasseter received a Special Achievement Award for his leadership.

In 2006, Pixar released *Cars*. Lasseter **directed** the film. That same year, Walt Disney Studios bought Pixar. Jobs asked that the two companies remain separate. He also wanted Catmull and Lasseter to lead both companies. Walt Disney Studios agreed. Catmull was made president of both studios. Lasseter was made chief creative officer and executive **producer** of all films.

THE BEST OF
BOTH WORLDS

Disney's **animators** were excited about the new direction their company was taking. Pixar's employees were more hesitant. They worried that Pixar would become a copy of Disney. But Lasseter and Catmull handled the change with great leadership. They were able to move forward while preserving the magic of each company.

Pixar's inventive spirit influenced the atmosphere at Walt Disney Studios. At Pixar, Lasseter had developed a group called the Brain Trust. This was a group of **directors**, artists, and others who met to discuss films in progress. At Walt Disney Studios, Lasseter created a similar group called the Story Trust. The group encouraged employees to speak up and share ideas.

Lasseter (*left*) and Catmull (*right*) at the premiere of Disney-Pixar's *WALL-E* in Los Angeles, California. The film was nominated for six Academy Awards.

Elsa, the ice queen in Disney's *Frozen*. At its 2013 release, the film made more than $1.2 billion worldwide.

As creative officer and executive **producer**, Lasseter kept very busy. In 2009, Pixar's *Up* was nominated for an **Academy Award** for Best Picture. That same year, Lasseter won the Golden Lion Lifetime Achievement Award for his work in film. It was a tremendous accomplishment.

Pixar and Walt Disney Studios grew more successful with each film. Lasseter directed Pixar's *Cars 2*, which released in 2012. The film received a **Golden Globe Award** nomination. And in 2013, Disney's *Frozen* further proved just how popular an animated movie could be. It became the eighth best-selling film of all time. Lasseter, *Frozen*'s executive producer, called it "one of the most beautiful animated films ever made."

CRITICS 👍 REACT 👎

"I blow a **piston** whenever 2006's *Cars* gets trashed as the **runt** of the Pixar litter. . . . *Cars* may not match *The Incredibles*, *WALL-E*, *Up*, and the Toy Story [films]. But *A Bug's Life* sure eats its dust. I could go on, but *Cars 2*, number 12 in the Pixar hit parade, should end the **debate**. [It] is a tire-burning burst of action and fun with a beating heart under its hood."

—Peter Travers,
Rolling Stone

"It actually hurts to knock one of [Pixar's] movies—something I've never done before. . . . *Cars 2* is so cluttered and confusing it's actually hard to follow, right up to the end. . . . It never stops moving; you just don't know where it's moving, or why."

—Leonard Maltin,
Indiewire

The writers both reviewed *Cars 2*, but their opinions are very different. Consider both sides. Who makes a better argument? Do you agree with one review more than the other? Why?

ON THE SET OF
CARS 2

Every day is a busy day for Lasseter. After all, it takes a lot of work to make a movie! Lasseter starts each morning very early. A driver brings him to Pixar headquarters in Emeryville, California.

This gives Lasseter an extra hour to work. On this particular day, he reviews the lighting on some *Cars 2* **clips**.

Lasseter arrives at Pixar with a big smile on his face. He offers a hug to each coworker he greets. Lasseter compares his work as a **director** to being a cheerleader. Pixar's executive manager and production manager plan his full day.

First, Lasseter watches some film clips called **animation** dailies. He suggests a timing change

Lasseter combined his love of cars and spy films to create this action-packed sequel.

Daniel Whitney, the voice of Mater, made up about 20 percent of his lines while recording.

to make the **lines** more realistic. Next, he reviews a new musical **score**. He doesn't think it works very well. He instructs the team to use the original score.

Lasseter also attends a sound meeting and a lighting review. He approves some **clips** from the **special effects** team. At every step, he makes suggestions to keep the story focused and engaging. And after ten hours at work, it's time to head home. Lasseter returns to Sonoma, California, for dinner with his family.

TODAY &
TOMORROW

Lasseter continues to keep busy at work and at home. He and Nancy have five sons, Bennett, Joey, P.J., Sam, and Jackson. When he's not at home, Lasseter is busy working on new films. Pixar and Walt Disney Studios always have several films in production. And Lasseter is the executive **producer** for each one. In 2015, Pixar released a new original movie, *The Good Dinosaur*.

Despite his busy schedule, Lasseter still hopes to **direct** more films. And he will always be interested in new storytelling

FUN HOUSE

The Lasseters' home in Sonoma, California, is full of fun surprises. It has a hidden staircase and model train library. The Lasseters also own a nearby winery, which they opened in 2002.

Lasseter and his family at an awards ceremony in Los Angeles, California. Lasseter was awarded a star on the Hollywood Walk of Fame.

technology. He is famous for saying, "It's not the technology that entertains people. It's what you do with the technology."

The future of **technology** may be a mystery. But it's almost certain that Lasseter will continue to inspire smiles and laughter. Lasseter's talent encourages artists young and old. His **passion** for storytelling shines through in every movie he touches.

TIMELINE

1957
John Lasseter is born on January 12 in Hollywood, California.

1973
Lasseter tours Walt Disney Studios for the first time.

1979
Lasseter graduates from CalArts and begins working at Walt Disney Studios.

1983
Lasseter experiments with computer animation. Disney soon fires him.

1984
Lasseter helps create the first computer-animated short film at Lucasfilm.

1986
Lasseter writes, directs, and animates "Luxo Jr."

FAMOUS WORKS

Toy Story
Released 1995

The first ever full-length computer-animated film.

Nominated: Best Original Song and Original Screenplay, Academy Awards, 1995

Monsters, Inc.
Released 2001

The first Pixar film to win an Academy Award.

Won: Best Original Song ("If I Didn't Have You"), Academy Awards, 2001

Finding Nemo
Released 2003

This film became the best-selling DVD of all time.

Won: Best Animated Feature Film, Academy Awards, 2003

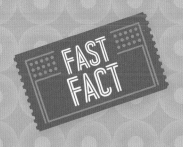

FAST FACT

From 1989 to 1991, Lasseter directed commercials for Tropicana orange juice, Listerine mouthwash, and Life Savers candies.

1988

John Lasseter and Nancy Tague are married.

1996

Lasseter receives a Special Achievement Award for his work on *Toy Story*.

2002

Lasseter and family open a winery in Sonoma, California.

2006

Lasseter becomes chief creative officer for both Pixar and Walt Disney Studios.

2009

Lasseter wins the Golden Lion Lifetime Achievement Award.

2015

Lasseter announces his role as director for 2017's *Toy Story 4*.

Cars
Released 2006

A family road trip inspired Lasseter to write this story.

Nominated: Best Animated Feature Film and Best Original Song ("Our Town"), Academy Awards, 2006

Up
Released 2009

The first animated film to open the famous Cannes Film Festival in 2010.

Won: Best Animated Feature Film and Best Original Score, Academy Awards, 2009

Frozen
Released 2013

The first Pixar film to focus on a female main character.

Won: Best Animated Feature Film and Best Original Song ("Let It Go"), Academy Awards, 2013

29

GLOSSARY

Academy Award – one of several awards the Academy of Motion Picture Arts and Sciences gives to the best actors and filmmakers of the year.

animation – a process involving a projected series of drawings that appear to move due to slight changes in each drawing. An *animator* is a person who creates a work using this process.

bonus – something that is unexpected but welcome.

clip – a short piece of a movie or television program shown by itself.

computer graphics – the pictures or images that can be made on a computer.

dealership – a business that sells a specific kind of product.

debate – a discussion or an argument.

direct – to supervise people in a play, movie, or television program. Someone who directs is a *director*.

engineer – someone who is specially trained to design and build machines or large structures, such as bridges.

enroll – to register, especially in order to attend a school.

Golden Globe Award – an award recognizing excellence in both the movie and television industries.

lines – words that actors speak in a play, movie, or television program.

passion – great devotion or enthusiasm. Someone who has much enthusiasm is *passionate*.

piston – a cylinder fit inside a hollow cylinder in which it moves back and forth. It is moved by or against fluid pressure in an engine.

WEBSITES

To learn more about Movie Makers, visit booklinks.abdopublishing.com. These links are routinely monitored and updated to provide the most current information available.

pitch – to present a movie or program idea for consideration.

premiere – to have a first performance or exhibition.

producer – someone who oversees staff and funding to put on a play or make a movie or TV show.

runt – the smallest animal in a group that is born to one mother at the same time.

scene – a part of a play, movie, or TV show that presents what is happening in one particular place and time.

score – music written to accompany a play or a movie.

screening – an event in which a movie is shown to a group of viewers.

sequel (SEE-kwuhl) – a book, movie, or other work that continues the story begun in a preceding one.

special effects – visual or sound effects used in a movie or television program.

technology – the use of science to invent useful things or solve problems.

3-D – short for *three-dimensional*, or having three dimensions, such as length, width, and height. Something that is three-dimensional appears to have depth.

twin – one of two children born at the same birth to the same mother.

winery – a place where wine is made.

INDEX